CSU Poetry Series LXI

The
Saint of
Letting
Small
Fish
Go

Eliot Khalil Wilson

Cleveland State University Poetry Center

Acknowledgments

Grateful acknowledgment is made to the editors of the following magazines in which some of these poems first appeared, sometimes in slightly different form:

Beloit Poetry Journal, Blue Mesa Review, The Carolina Quarterly, The Cimarron Review, Cutbank, Mid-American Review, Flyway, The Green Hills Literary Lantern, Green Mountains Review, The Journal, Many Mountains Moving, Margie, The MacGuffin, Mudfish, The Nebraska Review, Nightsun, North American Review, Onthebus, Parnassus Literary Journal, Phoebe, Ploughshares, Slate, The Sonora Review, The Southern Review, Spinning Jenny, The Spoon River Poetry Review, Washington Square, West Branch and *Willow Springs.*

"Designing a Bird from Memory in Jack's Skin Kitchen" was reprinted and produced by Born Magazine in collaboration with flash artist extraordinaire Rick Mullarky.

I would also like to thank Josh Bell, Steve Fellner, David Floyd, Abraham Smith, Karen Broucher and the Portlandia Group, Simone Muench, Ander Monson and Paul Guest, for his friendship and inspiration.

Special thanks to Joel Brouwer and Bruce Smith.

Published by Cleveland State University Poetry Center
2121 Euclid Avenue
Cleveland, OH 44115-2214
www.csuohio.edu/poetrycenter

ISBN: 1-880834-58-8
Library of Congress Catalog
Card Number: 2002114908

The Ohio Arts Council helped fund this program with state tax dollars to encourage economic growth, educational excellence and cultural enrichment for all Ohioans.

The
Saint of
Letting
Small
Fish
Go

*For my mother and father
and for Sophia*

Contents

The Fine Art Women of Belsen

from the USHMM photo archives

Any likeness,
a profanation,
but being
at once alive and dead,
wren-tiny,
totem-thin,
delicate past touching,
they're like
Giacometti's women.

Consider the lines
their bodies make—
the folds
of clothes,
the projection
of bone
and muscle—
whispered exclamations
against wire lines—
shrinking,
smaller still,
reduced to
their viable limits
and moving in
upon themselves,
a closing book,
a wrinkled brow
in concentration.

Still the faces—
Giacometti knew them
as indivisible,
unified as water.
This is what tortured him,

having only the artist's
subdividing bronze and clay.

The task—an apple—
from a tube of Mars red.
From words—mercy—
that familiar foreign country.

Syrian Light and the Leisure of Moths

This must have been how it was
to look down from the orchard hills of Ghota at dawn,
and see Damascus shining far below
and for the last time.

In that light, it must have looked fragile and clean
like acres of card houses.
He had what he could walk with—
the *piastres* for his ticket,
flat bread for the slow passage, a folded
name and address.

But this isn't the honeyed light of memory; it's coal dust
from the number three shaft mine in Clearview, West Virginia,
drifting through the windows and doors,
mapping the palms of his small, brown hands,
following him into the house where his wife
is raising nine children and living at the stove
with her ginger root fingers and her cabbage heart
        the leaves of which she gives away.

She was a cool round washing machine
        wearing a feedsack apron.
He was a lunch pail and beard full of coal
        gone to the mine with the night's last shadow.

Weaving ruined nylons into rugs,
hunting dandelions in spring,
scraping the bones of dinner
into the black dirt of the garden,
they never owned a car, or flew on a plane,
or tasted store-bought eggs.

What was he thinking the night
I found him watching the listless way

the gypsy moths kept flopping their wings against
the screen, a dozen opiated concubines,
each of them yawning and waving a fan?

The Syria that was left for him was in his fig and apricot trees.
Haunting no one in the paid-for house,
settled, but half-homeless
until the breath in his black and clouded lungs
refused to move.

Elegy for the Twice-Invisible Body of Jesus Blanco

To travel up from warm Nueva Rosita,
to be found frozen in the parking lot of Sears
among flattened cans and empty carts
by the dollar-plumbing mall walkers.
Was the irony hot or cold for you?
To die homeless in such opulent proximity.

I've heard it called *a failure of lifestyle*—
—the downside of your buffalo freedom—
the sad B side of democracy.

But, Jesus Blanco, I'm going to let you in,
spread the net of American possibility over you,
grant you advertised trousers,
pastel bath coordinates,
drapery, pantryware
and the ecstasy of room temperature.

If you are invisible even now,
even to other ghosts,
then a new fragrance,
popular sunglasses,
a German razor.

You would do well, Jesus Blanco,
not to notice how at dusk each of these winter nights
the starlings arrive in the parking lot—
solely, brokenly, brawling with their tiny dinosaur brains,
but centripetal even so.

It's something akin to faithfulness—
how they number from covey, to swarm, to congregation,
—a benevolence in their almost human noise—
their flight—en masse—a living smoke.

The Bucket of No Sympathy

There was never money for pots or traps.
We'd meet the high tide with our poor magic,
tie turkey and chicken necks to kite string,
and watch them sink into brown-green water—
        like crescent moons drifting down and away.

Then we crawled sideways along the bulkhead
and waited all day like threadbare spiders
for lines to move, to ouiji ghostily,
there where my brothers and I had tied them
to the bulkhead or the NO CRABBING signs.

The youngest, I would pull the crab line in,
a skill of privilege, the Clotho of Crabs,
a straight line needs a slow hand-over-hand,
        not so fast or slow to scare it away.
You learn to judge the crab's heft and hunger—
how to move as sudden-slowly as age—
and how to keep your shadow off the line.

You pull the line—a dim incandescence—
—the chalk-white carved and tiled underside—
and then the whole manifold jewel of it:
its carapace, a wet slate and moss agate,
its two claws, an opulent Parrish blue,
a blue like nothing else from that river,
and tipped with tyrant and martyr red.

Most cling until they're half out of water.
You can see their eyestalks twitching and watch
their plated mouths open and close sideways
like a professional shuffle of cards.

But the claws are what I remember best.
The locked stubborn clutch, the certain fury,

mocks me in each of my bloodless defeats.
What have I held past thoughts of letting go?

A claw might be wrenched out of the socket
and continue to bite in such a way
that years later the image still props up
my memory of the word *bellicose.*

They would have to be ripped from the crab net.
They might bite through a tennis shoe before
being picked up between their paddle fins—
she-crab, doublers, and blue Jimmies alike—
and dropped into the bucket where they'd brood,
bubble morosely—biting each other.

It so suits them—their cardinalization—
their red bodies no better epitaph.
Still, when dropping them into the boiling
water, a daisy chain of claws, it was
too hard not to think there some softening—
such pinching, grabbing becoming a hold.
Harder still when they'd scratch the pot's wall
a so-quiet scratching, unbearable
without some prior benefit of pain.

        One of us would have to be bitten.
(This one of many boy-blood rituals.)
There had to be a mark. We'd alternate.
Poor or not, cruelty needed reason then—
                this, many years before the draft cards came,
                and before the Kepone killed the river.

A moment's eternity. Crouched before
the pail, my brothers witnessing the rite,
a left hand—that was each of our left hands—

the torpid-seeming bucket of livid crabs
a left thumb just over the bucket's rim
then the splash, and a crab not letting go
then the panic, the shaking and cursing,
and a hand that bled and bruised over.

       Only then could we drain the stale water,
cut lines, and walk home, the high tide leaving
—already gone—and our backs to the moon.

Designing a Bird from Memory in Jack's Skin Kitchen

We hated everything below us.
We'd come to hate the ground itself,
to dread the heavy ropes of gravity
drawing us down from blue
to a brooding green
which would billow in tan dust
like waves of fistic clouds.

We'd come to kill
the afternoons, to evade
the blanket heat by flying out of rifle reach
and dropping mortar rounds through the clouds and trees,
our demented resentment
entirely non-personal.

I would come to forget Isaac,
our Arab gunner, with his shell carton filled with baklava
and just how mixed he was
bearded, but awash in after-shave,
dropping incendiary bombs and Hershey bars at the same time,
Viet S'mores we called it.
How he could shoot his .50 caliber, stoned on hash,
as accurate as fate itself.
How he'd shoot children and dogs,
but not women or birds. *Bad luck*,
he said. *Even when they are dead,*
women and birds remember.
I would forget how we found him later in Song Ngan Valley
        mixed with the ground and chopper,
repatriated, tangled like a lover,
his broken hand up and open
as if feeling for rain,
or patiently expecting some small gratuity.
The visor of his helmet shining the same

blue-black iridescence
as the glass of Chartes cathedral.

Right here, I tell the tattoo man
giving him my arm,
A blue bird, that certain blue, with black eyes
and rising.

The Forbidden Channel

Freud was right; we are such bad citizens.
Born febrile, remorselessly sexual,
and cut from that one principle we keep.

How he'd love these late-night half-blocked channels.
The vertical lines pinching, contracting
and pulling a "*God, yes!*" from the scramble,
from this blooming kaleidoscope of skin.

That's you; that's what you are, a mirrored web,
a body of hands, a small Hindu god.
Everything, everything, your reflection.

In this filtered field of objects and part
objects appearing and disappearing,
even interference is erotic.

And singularity is taken off.
Manifest breasts of some silver co-ed
warp and curve into two latent pillows.

The mouth of her Daguerrean roommate
throbs like a pulse then quickly vanishes.
The white couch's arm bends into a thigh.

The in-and-out sound of a slow-motion
shower is that same sound of one hand cracking
an egg into the empty face of a pan.
Life consists of such naked suggestions.

Late at night on the forbidden channel
even darkness is not the final dark
just the floating dark of before you were born.

It's true. What's clear and certain leaves us cold.
No other channels. What could replace this?
And turning it off means you disappear.

New Orleans Odalisque

from a line by Simone Muench

Always the curved shape
between the sight of sweetness and its taste,
she's the eye's frottage, the Ideal Form,
and the hours that brought me here
have left me.

In this place I can make believe—
believe her name—Desire—my second favorite abstraction.
Believe this fireman's pole is what's left
of the playground of her Catholic school,
and that she must be its most wayward charge—
black skin as smooth
as the inside of a milk chocolate egg,
a tea towel of a pleated tartan skirt
above the bunched silk garters
where the dull green flames of bills lick at her legs.
She wears the sheerest of button-less blouses
then not even that.

And I am unrepentant Acteon,
fixed and unblinking for this
Diana un-appareled.

She twists like a flame.
Her back, a sierra of bone,
her hips, a sandstone canyon.
And I can believe her gaze,
born from a thousand years dreaming
and as dew-cool as moonlight,
is only for me.

She is married to so much:
to the heart's allegretto, the lightning bug's flare,
the spin cycle tremors, the scented arms,

the bass-rattled windows of prowling cars
to the Navy men who drift in and scuttle away,
the Korean tourists with eyes like wet mouths,
the students who watch like starving lions—
an imminent, plain-stilling stare—
to the heat of the sidewalk of Bourbon Street
moving up your thigh
like a tongue of hot air.

Cosmic Bowl

We took time in our bowling bags
and wished on ebonite and karma
        to strike a red-tipped white carnation
                at the end of our lane
to break the teeth of our paper mill jobs.

Raising Jupiter,
transcendentally smashed,
we bowled in the hardwood wheat field.
        Deep in beer, drinking on
            the way a half-ruined thing cries out
to be utterly ruined.

And we didn't leave.
And we didn't want to leave
        the timpani roll of what-happens-next
            which is not the sound of the linerboard machine
or the pressure screens or the empirical pulper.

On our own time, what we make happen,
that season of no season,
rolling towards the un-mystical bald dawn,
with bubbles from the bottom of our beer glasses
speeding up to the white foam as if
in sympathy.

Earl and the Ballerinas of Clark Hall

Each year they come for the ballet intensive
in pairs or pairs of pairs,
clean like I've never been,
slight and polished, but strong,
with faces like French words
and pour down around me,
move down the stairs
of the high-windowed rehearsal hall
and out into the early evening
like a stream of bloom.
    And when in pink, these crepe myrtle girls
    shame all that isn't flowering now.

I'm for the wastebaskets and the polished floors
—cleaning most of the night—for more than twenty years.
The bathroom mirrors show my hair all gray.
I am pinned in the puzzled accident of old age.

I might live beneath the building,
dragging a dead leg up the stairs
to ring some frightful midnight bell.

Like the campus' abandoned cats,
I am tuned to darkness.
Used to afterness, echoes, garbage.
    Whatever is left to find.

Once a crepe myrtle girl thought
I was waving to her. She waved back to me,
not seeing the rag in my hand
      for the window I was cleaning.

Earl at the Food Paradise: Sample Day

All those I had lived to never try:

southern rose apples, galas,
mineola oranges, canary melons, quince, comice pears,
Rainier cherries, papaya, jack fruit, marion berries, mission figs,
and though I'd heard it called stealing,
and often remembered seeing police cars waiting outside,
and even walked by cops as they tried to interrupt explanations—
        Ma'am . . . please listen . . . but Ma'am—

I bit into a Paula Red apple,
peeled a blood orange and ate from the young breasts of mango.
I sampled the white flesh nectarines, the testicular kiwi, green plums,
the slightly disappointing passion
and star fruits.
Feeling all of it partly mine.

And people watched.
As I leaned against the pickle barrel,
halving a miraculous geode cantaloupe,
They waited their turn and slice,
then drifted off to eat from the bakery.

Near the back of the store
Uncle Brownie, as I remembered him, had set up his hibachi
and was handing out grilled croaker and spot.
My mother was there with the card table up,
and in her domed Sunbeam electric skillet,
in a bubbling sea of fat,
were the fried eggs of memory,
crispy-edged, volcanic
and tasting exactly like
everything.

Then I remembered what I had come for
—my gallon of milk.
I reached for it.
The milk turned warm in my hands,
pink, then a bright new red.

Blank Verse for the Leaving Season

You would not help and even robins knew.
They waited on the fence, impatiently,
for me to tire, but I'd a mind to dig,
so I turned the red clay and riverrock
until my hands were swollen, blistering,
until the soles of both feet ached and burned.

Last March we dug this garden together.
Tomatoes going where tomatoes go,
the peppers going where the peppers go,
and the ground writing its name on our knees.

You might've stayed the spring, for the flowers:
The zucchini shedding their ruffled skirts,
the vascular mint, spreading and spreading,
the moonflowers closing their spiraled hearts,
       whenever the late sun turned ungracious.
You could've waited for the snapdragons
or for the sake of the white onion sets
       they wait—patient as an empty room.

You'll miss the globe basil's blooming spires:
       the finials of Chinese temples.

       If I thought it might bury or reveal,
I'd dig a mine or some grave distance,
dig until a kimono sky breaks through,
and I am beset by startled Asians.
But it's growing dark, even where you are.

The Black-Shawled Widows of Castilla y León

step from clamorous hives of tenement houses
and walk the grafted sycamore alameda,
two slow, dark seasons of belief.

They've come out for the night's paseo,
pulling their market carts, question-stooped, cobbled hand in hand,
with bread for the pigeons still, and spit for the bust of Franco.

They walk to the stork-priested cathedral,
and I've seen what walks behind them.

I no longer expect to see the winged heads
of powdered angel babies, rose-cheeked and corpulent,
hovering high above the traceries, pulling golden chains.
Nor do I wait for an immaculate wind
to stir a palette of silver clouds into a thunder annunciation.

But how I want these widows to pull their market carts
through the carved portal and feel the cathedral,
that summa of faith in light and stone,
first sway like a line of boats at harbor,
then lift into the air.

Let this happen not finally but at last.
The holy husk, fueled by how many centuries of votives,
has waited to rise,
to lift from its buttresses and ashlars, a prismed balloon,
and gather the widows up
into all of light's vocabulary.

At last, it should rise above the plague
of mopeds and florid tourists of the coin-operated world,
ascend in some infinite direction

up where the night-summoned stars pulse and parry.

But let it drift back down and cover the tombs
that faintly read *aqui espero*—
though the rest is worn away.

Let it settle back on its foundations,
bringing back the impassioned widows,
at that dawn moment when objects drift back into themselves,
and the great rose window returns whatever light the stars have tithed.

Ode to Necks

Here is a heaven of swans—
stone-smooth—
soft as the petal skin of eyelids.

Here is that
that says I have thought too long with my hands,
worked too many years in the actual,
      am overly apprenticed in the matter of fact.

So now when I hear Father Elias say
The soul lies midway
between the mind and the body,
I picture the neck.

And not only the neck of Christ at crucifixion,
a tan canyon range rivered with blood,
—straining like a weightlifter—there on my Mexican votive—
but any neck—
any place between the bone helmet of skull
and the carapace of torso—
be it slender-green like a poppy stem,
bristled and tendonous like a sunflower,
or trunk-thick and muscled—
Hermosos y bravos—
like the gleaming necks
of the Plaza de Toros.

How all the world is braced on seven bones.
The so-needed avenues
jacketed like an ear of corn.

Think of the giraffe women of Burma
with their towering brass ring necks,
threaded like light bulbs,

safe from gravity's tugs and tigers.

O, how I love the soulful neck,
the essential column.
Faultless ebony,
wattled and pelicaned,
or creased and white as a stack of hotel towels,
this the softest visible skin.

Don't I know the guillotine's appetite,
Dracula's splintered heart?

This morning was the cathedral white neck
of the young house wife in front of me.
Like a sudden wolf,
I'd rout this flock of appropriate churchgoers
if I let my lips graze the nape of her neck
the nuddle—there
just below the down of fine black hair
that smells of rain on summer-heated streets.

I'd press my lips to her neck
and know what the ear knows from the whirled conch—
the blood's well, the heart's strict iamb,
echo of an evening hymn, promise, and sleep.

Wedding Vows

...and I'd like to add that I will mind like a dog. I will wear whatever you like. I will go wingtip. No more white socks. A necktie stitched to my throat, turtlenecks in August. New York gray or black, only colors that dogs can see. I will know of squash, vermouth, and wedges. I will do all the grilling because I love it so. I will drive the wagon, man the bar, weed-whack compulsively. I will make money, the bed, never a to do.

I will build like an Egyptian, a two-mile pier complex, a five-story deck. I will listen like a bat, attend to the birth of sounds in the back of your throat. I will remember like an Indian elephant, recall requests made of me in a previous life. Your date of birth will be carved in the palm of my hand. I will make good. I will do right. I will sleep on the pegboard on the wall in the garage.

I'll have a tongue like a sperm whale, eyes like a harp seal, biceps like a fiddler crab. I will have gold coins, gold rings, stiff gold hair like shredded wheat. I will be golden at receptions, gold in your pocket, Paganini in your pants. Money will climb over the house like ivy. Excellent credit will be my white whale. I will always. I will everyday. I will nail the seat down. I will let you pretend I am your father.

I will be a priapic automatic teller machine, never down, never a usage fee, a stock prophet, a para-mutual seer, tractable, worshipful no matter what. I will always want to. I won't notice what you don't point out. I will entertain your friends, say how your love saved me. I will convince them. I will talk, really talk, to them. Deep meanings will be toothpicked and passed around.

I will need zero maintenance. I will be a utility or a railroad. There will be no breakdowns or disconnections. I will allow you lovers, Moroccan teenagers and Turkish men. I will adopt them. I will not cry. I will respond to grief by earning more. My sweat will smell like drug money, like white bread baking. I will be as clean as a Mormon, wholesome like Iowa. I will lead. I will be a star, a rock, like Rock Hudson.

Someone Else Happy

The day before my wife said she'd leave,
I took our daughter to the Salvation Army,
where everything comes in that same smell.

She is enchanted by the wonderland of bric-a-brac,
and anything reachable becomes a moment's toy.

It is wonderful for me too.
The stacks of stained traveled luggage from
the Hotel Savoy Majestic and the Dresden Paladium,
the cracked plates, the de-nuded ornaments,
the single shoes, and torn quilts,
pluck at my instinct to rescue and preserve.

I can't though.
These things are here for a reason,
and in each chipped cup I hear that thought
that considered, then dismissed it.

I never use it.
It will make someone else happy.

After all, I am here to add
my fragments to this space,
purging the house of remnants:
all that's mismatched, the broken frames,
the ruined ties.

I find my daughter flying an F-14
through rows of weary sweaters.
Her left hand holds a naked armless doll up to me.
It's nice, I tell her,
but it can't come home with us.

Pueblo Eterno

I've gone back to where I might have left it,
searched the blaze azaleas, the March plum trees,
looked under the smell of bread and coffee,
thought it there where a man sings to his dog.
It's there: the flour-white Mexican town
of love's first, shy, and pure imaginings,
a place the years don't go. There I'm Pedro
with Steinway-black hair—in the right places—
dark skin to your liking, castanet eyes—
and no words. I speak Flamenco guitar.
And if shadows of hours stain and spread,
they serve the brilliance of our first light,
light that hasn't left us, but hovers still
in that Eden-clear and so blameless air.

Better than Beauty

For Sitto

You would not have amazed your Polish neighbors,
Frank and Alma Slanski, who were perhaps preoccupied
stealing garlic from your garden,
had you, to balance you, opened
your complimentary funeral home umbrella
with an uncustomary flourish and there,
with the low hovering fireflies for footlights,
in your housedress and your half-hose,
climbed up and walked the metal clothes line
up to the garden shed
and back again.

You would be on some errand.
Your twisted arthritic toes curved seemingly just for this.

Better than beauty is a camel

Cobbling slave work, queen will, and Arab magic,
you were as frivolous as dry shelter.
Raising the nine children and living at the stove.

Work is prayer

How like the Syrian proverbs in their obvious truths.
How plainly true and beautiful,
how pathetically given is what was offered:

Stairs are better than ladders
A man with one eye is not blind
After rain there will be nightfall

Pick a night in 1953 in Donora, Pennsylvania.
Under the bug-cluttered back porch light
your husband Leo is losing at cards

and fighting with Uncle Brownie or the priest or Frank or all three
or pontificating like only an happy Arab can:

All any man needs is a woman and some chickens

Your useful life, a labored absurdity,
in a blue-collar immigrant circus. This greatest show
went on in perpetual rehearsal and preparation
in the giant house, and was each year played,
in the coal dust and burnt onion air
for an older, smaller, less appreciative crowd
and then for the photographs and living room chairs
as even the neighbor's dog would sigh audibly behind the screen door
raising its head as if to smell the sound of other dogs.

I must wear my favorite suit,
have my eyelids glued shut,
my jaws stitched together
            for all to witness or approve.
I must be lockboxed and buried
            and be given a magician's benediction
to find you again.

Your oracular kitchen stove
calls me back to you.
Its tiara of blue flame.

Khalid the Prayer Rug Collector

I am told Aman will open his carpet shop in the city.
Let him peddle his goat rugs, his piebald kilims,
his machined war rugs, his salmon-ground flatweaves.
Turkey work! Almost ninety-nine percent of it.

What he knows he took from me
or I gave him as gift.
I gave him the face that will make a fair price,
taught him the eyes, the spoons of speech,
taught him that to say hello to a Bedouin
is already to lose a loaf of bread.
I brought him to the bazaars of Meshed,
showed him the roads of Taimani—
            the ones not to travel most of all.

East of Herat I am still well-known.
Always there is tea for me from Shindand to Farsi to Shahrak.
My hands recall the hands stretched out to me
            and the cold, and the fires I was brought to—
fires like beds of tulips I would want to hold in my hands.
I am of that wool. I am missed.
The Ghor Province is my warp and weft.

Yet I am too long in the trade.
I barter now with the children of my former friends.
With a permanent place and money enough,
I will teach myself contentment.
The rugs grow heavier.
My breath is reduced, my vision is reduced,
As is my entire inventory of fine authentic
vegetable-dyed Baluch saddle bags, tent rugs, floor rugs and runners.

But all is not for sale.
I keep those rugs which are heaviest in prayer—
those with supplicant wear,

the small gloss, leaning to a shine,
where the knees of the pious kneeled
and the hands of Fatima rested around the mihrab
for the five times of prayer.

Such a rug was given to me
by an aged weaver in Tulak,
given near her death, in exile,
a *dja namez* of burgundy field and yellow palmettes
with meandering vines and a sea green border.

It brings a garden to my heart.
> *May God bring her to paradise*
> *and may she enter by whichever door she chooses.*

No, to prosper I will not kiss a dog on the mouth.
Should Aman have money to cleave the sea,
I will put down my envy
like a burden.

Blank Verse Directions to the Asylum Cemetery

for Arthur

First you would have to leave the rusted tracks,
alter your patterned cross-tie stepping, and
climb down through the railroad roses planted
years ago to help hold the rails in place.

Make your branch-bending way through a spinney
of blackberry and orange trumpet vine
to this clearing, this small un-level field.

Listen at this place and be Tillman Sills,
who smoked all day, who smoked all day long,
staring up through the metal grated window
like a netted fish.

Or Dozier Cade who heard spiders breathing
who heard fireflies ignite and blaze out,
who heard the motor drone of passing clouds,
and shadows spreading at him.

Or Ruth Brown, the baby blue patient gown,
pathless, out of mind, taking her good pans
wherever she was taken.

There will be a strict and orderly grid,
rows and rows of uniform depression,
rectilinear and evenly spaced
like a good, workable harmonica.

All beneath a sky—incurably gray.

This way won't be as hard as the way back,
this difference between getting lost and being.
But you asked me for precise directions:
                Die two times, and when you live, live this lost.

Breakfast at the Planet Diner

It's not Tiffany's
but here you can leave
the light gray rain of morning
and the sound of cars smoothing by
for breakfast noise,
the best of all human sounds.

A kind of chorus,
this angry grill,
the money clank of flatware
on a diamond green counter,
the clatter of sturdy cups and restaurant china,
hair-netted Betty talking-filling coffee,
singing George, the Greek, turning eggs,
pressing out waffles.

Here is everything stainless,
on a day that might begin,
as spotless as the open face
of a cool spoon.

And it's breakfast anytime,
so while Copernicus spins on his stool
before a carousel of syrup,
Oppenheimer stares down
at the warring atoms of his grits.

In our chrome and glass capsule,
we could have breakfast on the black ocean floor
or be quietly floating in space.

Amid the freemasonry of pancakes,
we are held in orbit below an over-easy sun,
the windows cloudy with human breath.

Meteoric Rise: A Consolation

Although hundreds of deadly meteor events have been recorded, the Hodges Meteorite is the only modern, known and authenticated instance of a meteorite striking a human in North America—Mrs. Hewlett Anne Hodges, Sylacauga, Ala, Nov. 30, 1954.

First, a myth, a misapprehension.
They do not rise, but fall, like all else,
to the blandishments of gravity.

Second, the issue of where.

Rest easy newlywed lawyers
hot air ballooning above Napa valley
hanging in the sky
like a sure-thing midway dart game,
almost too easy to be much fun,
the winds of the cosmos blow your way.

And never worry linen-jumpered Homewood women
who summer and Starbuck with plans for Prague,
brimstone is not the portion of your cup.
Go live as Lot left Sodom.

No part of you was ever among the Shansi Province poor
peaceably hoeing kohlrabi against the Mongol winter
and then the mortifying miracle—
          the red iron breath of a thousand dragons,
a killing rain of fire and thousands dead
in the furrows of their fields,
clay pigeons for the cosmic shotgun,
those who would have lived well enough with nothing
more miraculous than the sun and gentle rains.

Meteors have a libido for the poor.
The eye and its needle straight through their hearts
and homes and cattle and tender hopes.

Never some surgeon's gleaming Lexus,
but a Wheeling man's only working Ford
or Teheranian peasant's rug loom,
now a Romanian gypsy wedding party,
a water tower in Bangladesh,
an East German green house,
an Egyptian child's dog,

Then there is you, Mrs. Hewlett Hodges.
Stars do fall on Alabama,
a place famous for its targets,
and one of them fell on you.

Home and napping on the Herculon sofa,
then out of the afternoon blue,
a hole in your rented roof and ceiling
a crushed bought-on-credit Zenith
and a deep red lip stick blot on the vast expanse
of your tissue-white skin
from your belly to your hip.

And here the newspaper has you—
standing on the porch of your ailing rented house.
You're all shabby coat and horn rims
and holding the offending star
in your oven-mitted hand
like a failed lead casserole.

And what do the poor ever keep but their poverty?
I know God meant it for me, you pleaded to the judge
after all, it hit me,
but the man who owned the house took your star
having some better claim.

Now let's put your hands about the skull of the Earth

and feel as a phrenologist might,
free of both need and belief.
Feel the fatal pits and tell-tale depressions
There in Europe, Winslow, and the Yucatan.

Don't your fingertips recognize
the bite of that nuclear winter,
the acid rains, the dust and ash heaven,
and the innocent dinosaurs dead?
Ten thousand foot waves pound over
trailer parks and castle walls alike.

Tonight the trees keep the sound of that water
an echo, an adumbration.

So answer again, Mrs. Hodges,
magnet-boned sky queen,
Sylacauga's living Leda,
did you put on some knowledge with that power
or just some ice and bandages?

From Mourning to Morning

Pulvis et umbra sumus

The path sick sorrow takes passes through this place.
I was the night man, told to dress crow-formal,
to greet somberly, to point dismally, to look potentially sad

or vaguely pious. No smiling and—like the airport—
no jokes. In the break room, above the veneered dresser
where the shoe polish and pornography were kept,
a laminated poster gave the rules in black magic marker:

If you wear white socks with your suit, you will be fired.
If you have overnight guests, you will be fired.
If a casket is missing, you will be fired.
If you leave before being relieved, you will be fired.
If you fail to answer the phone, you will be fired.
If you tamper with the crematorium, you will be fired.

After nine o'clock, after I'd taken the widowed
and the un-consoled gently out by the elbow,
I was free to change or study or watch t.v.
or sleep or try to until morning.
Or stare at the bodies.
I held my breath to imagine their breathing.

Once I dreamed that a giant came and silently
wrenched the roof off the funeral home, and
the giant could not tell the difference between
the pointy, pale head-heavy corpses
under their sheets on their metal carts
naked as Mung bean sprouts,
and fresh from the examiner's perscrutations
and me.

With my first check I bought a cell phone,

kept it hidden like a pistol.
With call forwarding, the world was my funeral home.
I'd take the Cadillac hearse out on the interstate and open it up.
It rode like water off a stone.
I'd drive to Hardee's, drive down to the coal piers,
hear the river swell and breathe, the laughing gulls.

I quit before they fired me.

Spectacle

Jane the Human Nail, Shlitzee the Pin Head
rust in your in Florida trailer parks!
We've got cable TV—a human nature show
from our rented big-screened cathode nipple.

Some Fat Boy in a Big Daddy tee shirt
screwed his own sister—screwed her, we learn, twice.
The Fat Boy bleats, turns confrontational;
he lurches, while restrained, pushes, then screams:
  You want some of this, and, of course, we do.
  All those other men don't love her like me
  I don't hit her, at least, and I don't leave.

The audience roils like a pudding.
Jerry the Pious does well to keep peace,
until the leopard-skinned sister struts out
on the stage, there with her iodine tan,
spandex, pancake, and cotton candy hair.

The Fat Boy slaps her, and she slaps him back.
  He pinned me down like he did our mama.
  It was awful, small, his fat stank like beef.
  I'm therapized now—on medication—
  learning with my shrink about masturbation.

The audience—now all in innocent white—
stands on its seats, leans forward, burgeons up.
They are giants, lighthouse tall, some have wings
as the Fat Boy drains like a wound and shrinks
and shrinks. Now he is waist high in carpet
and leopard-skin sister treats him to her pump,
  stomps him like a fire in a public park.

The audience, that new sterling group,
is taller, cleaner and more pure of heart.
They savor the clues of what they are not
and drive righteously back to their lives,
back to their bright, newly functional homes.

Remedy

I need an old magnolia, bicep limbed.
Yes, glossy leaved, glinting.
Yes, a thunderstorm over me like a waterfall.
Nighthawks mothing in purple air.

I need the opposite of yesterday.
Anything cool mint green.
No part of a clogged civic artery.
Steady work and something lovely and moving
like women in airports.

I stay pajamaed and home for *Gunsmoke*
for clarity, the black and white hat moral law
and open my pre-approved mail.
    They love me. We're at first names already.
    Tell us more about you—
    I know where peaches grow that belong to no one.
    I have the good opinion of abandoned cats.

I need a drink and that girl image behind the bar,
her voice is the paused ringing feedback of hushed guitars
like a sound torn open,
like inside a wave.
Her lipstick, her lit face
looms up to me like up from dark water
What kept you?
then the music crashes down again.
I let that be my answer.

Just Now for Love and Collards

We should get up, and do as we planned
before that sun thickens the air with heat,
before it burns the dew from the dull grass.
The garden, it's true, won't tend to itself,
but just now, it's the temperature of dreams
as I watch the still-cool sheet rise and fall
and rise on the slope of your new belly.

Let the fennel have its lacey crown of seeds,
let clover and cheatgrass flourish and spread,
let kudzu strangle or drown in shadow
our new defensive line of marigolds,
let the globe basil bolt and spire,
allow the mimosa's diaspora.
What of it?

Just think of the green cutworm's devotion—
a piety you would have me destroy
by taking it from what it was born for
—that green lip for the tongue of collard greens
as close to what it loves as love allows.

Let it have what it loves—its brief green world.
Let the collards fill with holes, filigree,
let the inch worm make of them paper dolls,
let them be gapped and loose as bad knitting.
And spare us that saw about reaping what sown.
Are we Puritans? Is it weed or starve?

I'll bring decaf coffee and tangerines.
We'll watch the lace curtains tangle and belly
in the early June wind, and we'll wade into
the dizzy, waist-deep smell of gardenia.
It's necessary. Let's stay where we are,
just here and now, and grow wild.

Ella Says

She struck again her teacher said, my daughter, newly six,
like a fever or tantrum, a baby-hating fit.

At home her dolls all scalped and trashed
and today at lunch there's a gash

in the lip of the five year old neighbor.
Now this. Now I've that phone call to make, and I'm given over.

I am singled out. I'd hold up my hands
but to whom do I surrender? Her mother's sickness commands

a petrified response, all I can make and bear
to keep her last breaths from finding her.

Across town, in a semi-circle of lead-aproned men,
she drifts in the queasy sleep of radiation.

So I drive to pick our daughter up and hear the teacher say again
Ella seems to hate whoever is younger than she is.
She bites ears and scratches the kindergarten kids.

Does everything grow like cancer? I almost ask. What's become
of my own child, my honey lamb, my lizard girl is now a dragon?

A terror, a child Tyson, my child who was the meekest thing.
Ella says it's because of the *Lion King.*

Like a cake walk when the music stops or a child not picked to play
for being too old or lame or no reason anyone can say.

Ella says what's young will push her mother out of life.

Though I will be difficult to convince, the job should fall to Disney
to tell us both how that could never be.

Passion

I pounded nails through her creamy palms
and impossibly arched feet.
She never screamed, bled, or healed
—my breasted, blonde, pink Jesus—
—not a doll at all—but a gendered totem.

I had what you'd have to call a passion.

Before the microwave,
before the Whirlpool trash disposal,
I'd stuff her down the gaping mouth
of my father's mounted terror-eyed fish
so that only her white hair would show
in a narrative called *Barbie and the Rabid Bass*.

Or she would burn and melt in the furnace.
Her chemical skin blackening
in *Barbie: Virgin Bride of the Volcano*.

But I'd generally have her crucified.
My sister would find her, pull her down,
go weeping like Mary Magdalene
to my parents.

Always a new Barbie would appear in her cellophane casket
with her turquoise frying pan or a neon pink vacuum.

Zealous, I continued to nail her everywhere I could—
—the tree by the bus stop, under the grape arbor,
the telephone pole, out by the mailboxes—
but I couldn't save her.

Always my sister would pull her down,
and make her play her truly suspect games:

Give her to Kubla Ken, Sheik of the Sandbox,
who would rescue her from white slavery,
give her a patio, fashion shop, dream house.

A disdainfully rich and powerful man,
Ken would force himself upon her
in what you'd have to call a marriage.

Ginsberg's Ghost: Atlantic City

Ms. America you've given everything and now you're nothing.
5'4", 143 pounds, size fourteen dress, April 1, 2003.
Ms. America when will you stop wobbling and wear human shoes?
When will you fail to be eerily pleasant?
When will you stop having your breasts stuffed with sandwich bags
    of carcinogens?
Ms. America you made me want to be Pamela Anderson.
Ms. America when will you keep your clothes on?
When will you stoop to help the three stooped women on the 100-
    rupee note?
Ms. America when will you send your Spode and silver to a random
    address in Cuba?
When will you say that it doesn't happen to every man and it is a big
    deal?
Aren't you tired of being mostly hair, bleached teeth, and padding?
When will you stop aspiring to be an assemblage of gleaming
    cleavages?
Ms. America when will you rule your own womb?
When will you stop being sweet to the point of translucence?
When will you be demonic? When will you refuse to be interrupted?
Ms. America are you an unconscious victim only?
When you will admit that you've been interpellated by *Friends* ?
I love *Friends*. Everyone so perky. I watch it every chance I get.
Ross's monkey has vanished. It's sinister.

When will you say *I want* and *Fuck this* and *Fuck that* ?
Ms. America when will you be Mr. President?
When will you end this absurdly Pyrrhic war on drugs?
Ms. America when can we vote Texas off the island?
When will you blaze up and tell us that George W. Bush never
    happened?
He's embarrassing. I'm getting nostalgic for Richard Nixon.
From now on, *Je suis Canadien.*
When will you stop letting your emotional life be run by *Cosmo*
    magazine?

Are you a fun fearless female with flirty moves that floor him?
Do you know seven scorching sex tricks that make him ga-ga?
Ms. America come talk to me.

It occurs to me that I am Ms. America.
I am talking to myself again, and I miss my real lips.
I have to be orange.
My spirit feels overweight.
I need to learn to eat like the other mannequins
Don't speak to me. I'm having a beauty crisis.
I lash out with mascara now.
I can't go anywhere like this. I'm stooped and hairy.
I need a billboard's posture, emergency electrolysis.
Who will vacuum the fat out of my body?
This is all entirely too perverted and obscene for me.

Ms. America, I'd rather be dead.

Closer to Texas

Any day but Sunday,
they got the one-day bag of food—
        Cheerios, cans of fruit cocktail or amniotic peaches,
        field or navy beans,
        a tall white can with black letters that said,
        Beef or sometimes *Pork,*
        sometimes roll-on deodorant,
        maybe conditioner, sometimes condoms.
Always a three-day bag of food if there were visible children.
Then a change of clothes from the thrift store,
which, after scanning through, they'd usually refuse.

But what they wanted was the ten-dollar check for gasoline
to get them east to Birmingham
west to Meridian.

Sundays we're closed,
but I'm ass-deep in the donation bin
sorting out the yard sale overflow—
        King Solomon of bric-a-brac
        deciding at a glance between
        what is of value and might be sold
        and what should be hauled to the dump.

Sundays were dead as four o'clock,
but I liked the work. It brought my right mind.
And often in the trash bags of largess
there was unintentional treasure—
        washed bills in watch pockets
        a sterling earring mixed in among the others.

Then I heard their footsteps behind me.
He was a skinny man and young,
cigarette, Western hat and boots, NASCAR tee-shirt.
She might have been his daughter or his wife,

small and ginger cake brown.
His eyes looked for mine but I kept them from him.

>*We're needing money for gas to get her back to Texas,*
>he said, *I'm told this place has money for that—*
>beer and smoke on his breath.

Not much and not today, I said.
Anyway, it's a check that's only good for one tank
and can't get you where you need to go.
He listened, impassive, like not listening,
but what I said seemed like rain to her
and made me wish I hadn't said it.

I spoke to their backs,
You can help for pay.

Together we dragged out
stained mattresses, carpets,
and the leaking corpse of a waterbed.

I gave them cash and took their thanks
and saw them later, as I drove home,
my pilgrims,
leaving Texaco on foot,
a six pack in each of their hands
moving closer to Texas,
however they please.

Deer

I worked up in marketing at the paper mill.
He worked the pulper machine—
        a local man in a camouflage hat
with thick, relevant hands
who could take a ribbing for being
in my carpool while not actually having a car.

He lived the furthest out but closest to me
so I'd let him out last—
drop him off by his mailbox—
not willing to hazard the steep, rain-rutted road
to his house, as the road vanished
into a tangle of scrub oak and pine,
        but this day was threatening, so I turned
—and we bumped down the steep road
towards his house.

He asked again if I'd hunt deer with him—
said I could borrow a rifle—
a muzzle loader—to extend the season.
I drove and joked:

With me, it's a strike first
kill-or-be-killed scenario—like back in Nam.
I've got a black sawed-off 12 gauge called Affirmative Action
and I'm partial to shooting does especially while they're nursing—
meat's better— milk still on lips of the fawn.
        Either that or a flame thrower
or I heave grenades from the tree stand
so they're dressed out, more or less, when I get there. . . .

But the house,
the house was a struggle—
set back under the trees, wrong to the light, on a scab of clay.

Then a dog's sharp bark, the screen door's screech and slam
and from the windows, the mushroom faces of children,
children, and the clothes,
clothes everywhere, pinned to the wires,
the invincible red clay stains,
the wind rifling the aprons and pockets.

Ghazal: From Damascus to Donora

Not her eyes, not the remote abstraction of soul, but her fingers.
What music there was came through her fingers.

I knew her arms as tulip stems—as young as smooth.
But the ground always knew her pine root fingers.

And she knew the ground—what it had to give and wouldn't give again.
Knew most seeds as caskets that never grew back to her fingers.

Grafted to a black frozen city where the rivers burn.
She'd knead bread—as the dark brimmed blue—with her candlewax fingers.

Never that shape again—no wood grain or bone delta.
Only clouds, rococo—holding hook and eye—the blue, like her fingers.

A Farmer's Son Speaks of Leaving the Ground

Red clay wants to keep you.
Hold a handful.
See how it stains your hands,
your shoes, the cuffs of your pants.

And tell me I'm not a thing of this earth
though I left that way to live—
        the work from can't see to can't see,
the almost broke harrow and ailing planter,
the thrip-split cotton and the constant no rain—
    the stands capped for moisture—
but never rain
only wind falling
and the flightless heat.

I'm that
that will walk away from a drowning man
   from a thing in pain, from a house on fire—
      my own house—
for pavement—with new clothes,
with books, with the money he gave me
and pictures—

This one of the July melon field:
     My father, high up on the flatbed,
has yet to turn to catch the melon I've tossed up to him
               rising to stillness at apogee
and received in the worn-iron certainty
of knowing how to put things
so they won't move.

The Gradual All

The clear-water light of autumn is first
to go. Then, the detailed particulars:
the late sun on brick, the frost-feathered pane,
the aster blooming in the auburn field
of feed corn, blur as if poorly erased,
replaced by dishwater light of old snow.

Since the dark cloud shadows have come to stay,
squirrels run on air between telephone poles,
four dark birds, starlings or grackles or crows,
hover like distant un-moored ellipses.

And remembering Monet won't help you.
When he tired of the Rouen Cathedral,
grew bored with the hazy dim shadow-browns,
he'd feed his eyes lemons or coiled roses—
    all manner of vivid, articulate things.

Now you can't get close enough to your own skin
and the paint of the world will not stay in place,
and each morning more of the night remains—
bleeding in, clouding out the needed lines
and when those lines dissolve. . . .

When the streams of your eyes have flooded their banks,
holding your panic is fine art enough
and, regardless, you cannot see to run.

How the Picture Wants You Living

But there you are sitting up,
though leaning slightly on the arm
of the high-backed wicker chair,
and costumed so primly in your pleated black dress,
with your hands crossed to show your ring,
with your drugstored face,
and with those forever brand new shoes.

You were always a difficult child,
and here you are with your mother's mouth,
so plainly, not smiling.

So I think of the dark, trapped air
in the smallest organ pipe,
the one that dogs and maybe angels hear,
so small is the breath from its sad mouth.

And I think of the silent photographer,
stifling his customary requests
in the close dark of his shroud and
in light of your deep disobedience.

You with your eyes as open as any winter pond,
you who never even liked dolls,
exposing the camera's hocus-pocus.
You who are, so plainly, that
which has no illusions.

Sky Fishing

Mimicking wind, you rattle the branches
speak not at all and carry a big stick,
a broken bat or axe handle works best
though the tree will trade for a few pecans,
keep what it's offered like a fair exchange.
          Never throw what's valued or trust the limbs.

The man who owns the trees has left for church.
You watched his black pick-up cresting the hill.
He lives alone out of simple meanness.
Should he see you, he'll fire his shotgun
in the air and set his dogs upon you.
          You tear out like a page of the Bible.

You've croaker sacks to overfill with pecans,
crossbred Choctaw Giants and Stuart Grands,
          —what there is to bring home in November.

You have watched with a crow's disinterest
the zinc sprays in April and the good May rains,
noticed the lanceolate leaves unfurling,
seen the bud break, the long catkins hanging.
And seen, too, the readied folded sheets,
          the trunk shaker and pads set by the grove.

All year you've catbirded the old man's work
to slip between the shuck split and nut fall
          and play a thief in his green vaulted room.

You belly in where the rain has taken
the ground beneath the deer fence—a minute's work.
The highest throws bring the most pecans down.
Watch the bat with one eye, the branches
will twirl it like a baton and throw it

back at you in a hail of husks and twigs.

And though distracted, with your other eye
watch the pecans—they will football away
and hide under leaves for the squirrels to find
or the tractor's rake, and then to Dallas
to the factories, destined for fruitcake.

In the clear fall season of blue-gold days
you've four hours with the trees—fish the sky.

Once only you are here. The farmer will
come back from church to untie his dogs and
the hour will brim pink and start to blacken.

Come winter, whether rocked by boys or not,
every pecan limb and branch is bare.
        Look closely. You'll see country pecan groves
hung with broken broom sticks and tennis shoes,
bicycle rims, bats, or ruined paddles.
        There hangs a tale of deciduous things.

Blank Verse for the Man We Threw from the Sky

Though the memory doesn't feel like mine,
I must have been there, moving north north-west,
holding, up above the Perfume River,
with Simon, Isaac, our Arab gunner,
Vince, called Pineapple because of his face,
the NVA who kept on smiling
who would not stop to save his own life,
and Peter who had stopped asking questions,
having seen what no one should live to see
after Hue, and down to one emotion.

And if you could have held your head just right
seen the paint falling from the recent world
the old paint, there all the time, coming through,
you'd see our ancient nightmare carnival
framed in the CH-47's door
the Bosch pentimento of Viet Nam:

Here's child-meretrix selling her same ass
there in the tents which are huge green mussels.
The cargo choppers become dead-eyed fish
held down by the green bags of what remained
and the bodies, Jesus, pieces of bodies
women and boys in pieces, hanging in trees.
The dragons blowing their orange fires
with those same six hundred year old ravens
afterwards, and always a crescent moon.

But Bosch was wrong about how a man falls
in his *Descent of the Damned into Hell*
not handed to the air like a new bride,
or set down into space like firewood,
but arms out forward, braced, and on his knees
like a child's doubtful Indian dive,

but holding, past fear, and on both knees.

A parody of some liveable fall
with the river a lifetime below him.

The rest was just as Bosch warned us it'd be
and I'm not offended at our likeness:
demon-apes, empty of everything else,
prehensile hands, demon-hands, just like mine.

At the Used Book Store

You might as well be buried
in a hidden crater on the invisible moon of Venus,
but you are here—
left in the one-dollar box of books
outside an ailing used bookshop.
            Inside, the sci-fi and lurid bas-relief paperbacks
fly from the shelves,
but for you
the world has fishhooks in its pockets.

I pick you up,
scan the ruins of your verse,
your lavender words—your *lightsome breeze,*
your *perchance*—your *gay birds* and *soul*—
and I put you down.
            Not even the air of flight about you now.

And your maker who is long since dead?

She thought your boards
would keep a storm-pulling wind,
thought your spine would crack
to stirred chimes and the bread wagons of thunder
—your words strike through the cataract sky
but intimately, like the river's hands.

You are her faith in tulips,
almost the sum of her,
her seedling, fluid and ready, still.

Elegy for The Saint of Letting Small Fish Go

I.

You too might step into a puddle of fire,
or splash through a stream of glowing lava
where only moments before you were barefoot
in your kitchen after a late night of too much wine
and, nearly naked, frying bacon at the stove.

A burn like this is a different thing the doctor said
and I can believe it. I was a different thing.

I was a man with an unquenchable oil well fire on his feet
that would blaze up as the medicine ebbed.
And the skin curled over, brown-red,
too much like the meat I was cooking in the pan that I dropped
—an irony not lost on even the youngest of nurses
drinking and bacon don't mix
she kidded as I healed.

Yet had my wounds burned like Vulcan's forge
they'd be a distant fire in light of the child
behind the glass in the opposite bed.

II.

Where were you saints when the fire first licked his hands?
Hadn't he in living prayed to you?

I want the saint of ice cream trucks
to turn off the carnival, climb down, and explain it all—
        account for all the betrayers—
The saints of reachable branches and bank envelope lollipops,
the saints of his mother's cool arms, of new basketball shoes, and
professional wrestling.
The saints of tree forts, pocket knives, and stadium food.
The saints of waffles and eyebrows and box turtles.
The saint of jam.
The saint of his own bed.
Where were you saints of wheelies and rodeo clowns and rockets?

III.

I was at home when the sepsis took him
and they wheeled him to that all-light room
and when they covered his face.

Yet I had seen his grafts and debridements,
the twice daily baths and dressings,
and the shock at that last turn of gauze
— how the fire bit at his summer legs and arms—
black skin, blacker still, and red.

I was there to see the lost mother
who would live in fire for the child she had known.
There to see all who entered shake their heads
as if wondering as I wondered
how so small a thing can carry such pain
—pain that pushed through the morphine push—
—pain that conquered even those numbing Nordic gods—
Vicodin, Ativan, and Tylox.

It is not my place.
He was not my child,
and I could never speak to him,
but hold him out of the fire.
I would not have him burned again.

Give him back to rocking water,
to pendulum down through the fingers of the sun.
Let the ocean run his veins and heart—
            full, then empty, then full again.

Or return him to the folding ground,
face up to the sky.
A boon for dreamlessness,
this petty thief of time.

Saint Sophia: Map to Motive

Somewhere else—Thanksgiving.
Here there was no mail and no weather
if weather meant something other than rain
—it only rained.

We'd be thankful to seem the landscape,
parts of that rain-leadened jungle
our backs—banana leaves—
our helmets—mossed stones—
to be, in the ponchos they gave us,
a moving farm of Christmas trees.

But not if it meant
being part of that fucking ground.

And we could get anything—
steak sauce, Penthouse, ScotchGuard
anything—except dry and home.

Isaac got a photo still of
Sophia Scicolone,
but I knew her last name as Loren
a sound with a legend hinting.

The icon of our Nam Cosmology.

Both a rocket and a star,
transport and destination,
she was gravity's bright loss,
an image we could neither
reach nor renounce.

Our compass man determined
that her left breast
was larger than the right
with a westerly orientation.

But we were almost sick of bodies then
—too tired and weary familiar.
We zealots, can you believe,
worshipped her face.

Not the snow on marble face of Garbo
        but a face of more human music—
an earth-bound saint
with that harmony in curve of nostril
and the hieroglyph brows,
the simple crown of hair,
the bursting fruit of that mouth
and her great shrine-candle eyes.

A face that was to Nam
as cellos were to sniper fire,
as mortar rounds
were to mannered and literate silence
in cool, proportioned rooms.

A face enough.
Some map to motive, however far,
enough to keep us to our doomed pilgrimage
and have us lose our blood,
our lives, in places we couldn't pronounce.

And, so like a saint,
she is always absent
from my particular dreams—

dreams that were not dreams for many—
dreams where I live on point
with no rifle or radio or voice and
with no sound of rain to cover me.

Avec Tout les Fruits de Paris

The big cat had two worlds to rule and witness:
a dry wooded bushveld
with watchful kudu and forever sprung gazelle,
a baobab tree shading the distance—
        and, painted on the opposite walls,
a steep rock koppie
over the pattern of cinder blocks
and spotted with wattle and rock fig trees.

But the aging cheetah only slept.
Sleep, its only appetite,
in the worsening light
under the rusted chain link sky.

        For me, it's always the same zoo emotion—
        be it Paris, Melbourne, or Washington—
        a wonder close hunted by grief.

Now with a leftover bag of fruit
and half of one of two bottles of wine,
I move to the elephant pen
and call to the grey dune lying there.
Its vast corrugated and wind-carved skin
a relief map of some Jupiter moon.

Two low walls and a steep dry moat between us.

She creaks awake, rises like a surplus canvas tent,
and moves to me from her substantial sleep,
across her twenty yard horizon,
past her water trough and bales of hay
which are dulling from gold to gray
in the dust and winter weather.

How silent her underwater walk.

Her massive head directly before me,
her curved dull-pointed tusks
like sycamore limbs.

I hold up and toss a peach.
It bounces off her steep
forehead and into the moat,
out of reach.

At this she spreads her ears,
mirrored Africas,
and raises her trunk,
points it at me like a canon,
a mammoth *J'accuse.*

And I'm astonished to see
two small fingers,
pink and tender as any child's
at the tip of her trunk.

Je regret, I say—fluent with my elephant French—
and toss her a ruby nectarine.
It lands by the four delicate toes of her right front foot.

       She is all of dignity and deliberation.
       Whatever enters the pen can wait.

Then her trunk sweeps over the fruit,
lifts it, careless of dust and pit,
over her pink lips
onto the lavender tongue
in her ruminating jaw.

And didn't it please her tractable, gallon heart?

It's nothing, I said
but it might have been everything,
a passage, another sun,
the small ripe ministry of nectarines
        and with them the new grief of their absence.

I left not knowing if I'd return
or just how I'd be missed.
I gave her all the fruit that remained.

Last Day with Mayflower

I.

We slept on ripped quilts in the trailer's shade
or on pads in the cab between jobs.

The boss called us *backs*—our animal use—
and I was a *back* in the grey Navy town.

We sweated in the long pants they made us wear
but few of the men I worked with cared—
most had just come from state prison or jail.

This was a two-truck, no-piano move—
all a young housewife's things, bound for storage.
Her husband, dead and buried at sea.

We saw him in the newspapers we used
to wrap china and all the fragile things.
Dress whites, white smile, an Annapolis degree—
a crisp officer on a submarine.

He died in sunlight, a calm dry-ground day,
his jeep, his last dumb moment, and a train.
Now the house they bought became a train to her.
Their togetherthings became a train.

II.

That April I worked with Booze and Davis,
four-handed Booze our shoplifting king,
and Davis of sharpened screw-driver fame.
Davis was born tired and raised lazy.
They'd talk and laugh for ten hours a day.

I grew to like them—the way one can like
a man who lifts the other end of a dresser
or even takes the heavy end and walks backwards

down the stairs and up the ramp when you're sick
or too stoned or hung-over to lift much.

We were takers of sorts, a home turned house.
Making echoes by slow degrees
done when the house rang hollow and vast,
like the air inside a tire or a church.

III.
The young widow was beautiful that day
in her heavy grief and her bravery
and she was kind to us though we walked in
like children who'd been kept from all sadness,
singing, even, and blasting the radio,
to try and drown the dull work in music.

She'd stand on the porch and stare at the truck
with great blue red-rimmed eyes and then she would
bring boxes of china and books to the ramp.
She brought us cold water and sandwiches.

The last to be moved was the barber's chair.
It sat in the den, an enameled anchor.
Her husband's chair from his father's will.

IV.
She seemed to want to carry it alone.
She had tipped it on its side and pulled it,
all wrong, with her arms and it left a long
gash in the polished hardwood floor.
Next she hooked her fingers under the headrest
and pulled the weight against her chest
as one rows a boat or pulls a fishing net
until the blood in her arms and legs drained
and she dropped the chair heavily down.

How I wanted Booze and Davis to be quiet then.
I wanted not to have to ask them this.
Not to laugh at her in the hollow house.

This would be my last day, my first day, moving.

I should have said then—but how could I?—
that there must be a snow-quiet for her,
a slow quiet like the river tides,
the blue silence of a tired star,
the kind of silence that follows a train.

Tuscaloosa Knights: First Baptist Church

Let the spark-spreading wind begin,
let it bring the hay scent of storm,
let the red sun fall steeple-high.

Let the shadows from the waving row of cypress
that line the churchyard
mass and bleed across the road
to where a live oak,
the hanging tree, stood,
and a writhing fire roared.

When these tree shadows wave beneath
a righteous line of telephone poles
        with their long crucifix shadows falling far across
a common field of earth,
you would swear that shadows burn.

The same church windows,
the same high windows seem,
the absolute innocent elsewhere
of empty mirrors.

And though it says nothing
— word for word—
the mute church saw.

The Patrons of the Birmingham High Art Museum

And, yes, the museum should be moved from downtown,
to Homewood or Mountain Brook
some much closer, safer locale
away from the greedy park denizens—
that gnarled man with hands
like the feet of lame pigeons,
the shameless fountain bathers,
aluminum can addicts,
the solitary debaters,
the section eights, the lunatics.

About suffering they are not far along,
the young gentry.
Not for this do they arrive rather tarted up
bring their prosperous looking children
for an afternoon of arty play
and the *Guernica* scarf,
the Goya checkbook cover,
Starry Night thank you notes,
the Kahlo ice box magnets.

Then to the café,
the Tuscan pork chop,
Peruvian blue potatoes,
      Mozart and Gershwin play and play,
then candied violets,
the *crème brûlée*.

They pause a befitting length of time
before each and every redolent frame
and covet the dress of the Waterhouse *Ophelia*,
(that Gypsy look is in)
the Demuth *Five* for the family room,

the *Dove of Peace* for the den.

And didn't Bastien-LePage steal the show this year
with his *Harvest of October*—
the women at work, thin and clean,
happy in the limitless field,
the pink dawn of laughter in the harvester's face,
health in her Irish white hand.

The Common Dream of the Emperor Penguin

First a lone beta, its blue head full of thunder,
then a gold fish in a clear mixing bowl
a flecked and solitary swimming eye.

Then a pump, blue gravel, ten gallon tank,
a chatty chest with its necklace of air,
the cave-dark shipwreck, supine skeleton,
then guppies, black mollies, blue damselfish.

And by now my son will not hear of salmon
and there's no talk of fish sticks or tuna.

Since I will not fill the house with salt water
and swim to sleep with puffers and blennies,
we go to the New Orleans Aquarium.

He watches the tank of ghostly moon jellies,
the clown fish, the magic carpet sting rays
no-where eyed makos, all menace and teeth,
the Albino alligator, lolling,
like a piece of chewed gum.

He stares at the dragon-faced moray eels
until I can see them muscle and slide
into some crevice of his little brain
and ready themselves for tonight's nightmare.

But always the penguinary is where we end up.

We press the button and hear from the book
of their bright lives again. How it is that
at the pole, near where the south wind switches,
the male stands immobile, starving, through winter—
that unimagined, outer-space winter—

holding the one egg on the tops of his feet
until spring or longer when the mate returns.

We listen as more children come and press
their faces to the glass and now the room
teems with children transfixed by a new crèche
of downy penguin chicks and watchful parents.

Their preposterous barrel shifting walk,
their suits, such leapings and clappings
like fans at the end of an Italian opera.
Their visible lives
like listening to laughter.

The common dream of emperor penguins
is not so singular a thing as flight.

It is not among their formal hopes
to subdue and rule every element,
to missile through the black madness and dread
of deep water, then break from its weighty hands
to sail that other infinite acre
as fast, as high, as the sky laws allow.

The common dream of the emperor penguin
is fish and squid and peace enough for dreams—
like this little boy standing at my feet.

In the Argentina of the Mind

In the Argentina of the mind,
I never work at the mid-town mall.
Never work in some cell phone kiosk
selling minutes to my strange neighbors
like time is mine to sell.
Never dream of a house for us,
a garden for you, like any place
in this breathing might be ours to keep.

In the Argentina of the mind,
there are no cobwebs in your night-black hair.
Where would you have gotten them?
In the basement hiding Easter chocolate?
In the Daedalus maze of your imagination?
Certainly not from some office job.

In the Argentina of the mind,
we have the best possible rest
of our lives. There it rains when rain is wanted.
Wind presses the forest silver-green.

There I've a cabin and an arable acre for you.
You who are made from my dearest, lost,
Matchbox cars melted down for me.
You of the moon-glow yo-yo ears.
You of the lost cat's silent return.
You poppy in the corn.
You sparrow in the Wal-Mart rafters.
You summer hotel. You coffee.
You good mail.

I see you still set against a sheet
of Andean night.
Look, you say, *cobwebs.*
No, I thunder, *lightning.*